W9-CPE-568

WITHDRAWN

Time Is the
Longest
Distance

Other Anthologies by Ruth Gordon

Under All Silences: Shades of Love

Time Is the Longest Distance

An *Anthology of Poems*
Selected by

RUTH GORDON

A Charlotte Zolotow Book
An Imprint of HarperCollins*Publishers*

Time Is the Longest Distance
An Anthology of Poems Selected by Ruth Gordon
Copyright © 1991 by Ruth I. Gordon
Typography by Joyce Hopkins
1 2 3 4 5 6 7 8 9 10
First Edition

Library of Congress Cataloging-in-Publication Data
Time is the longest distance : an anthology of poems / selected by
   Ruth Gordon.
      p.   cm.
   "A Charlotte Zolotow book."
   Includes indexes.
   Summary: An international anthology of poetry about the
timelessness of time. Includes works by such poets as Emily
Dickinson, Rumi, Salvatore Quasimodo and Ono no Komachi.
   ISBN 0-06-022297-2. — ISBN 0-06-022424-X (lib. bdg.)
   1. Time—Juvenile poetry.   2. Children's poetry. [1. Time—
Poetry. 2. Poetry—Collections.]   I. Gordon, Ruth, date.
PN6109.97.T56   1991   90-4947
808.81'938—dc20   CIP
                                                              AC

To Ruth Anna Blank White—
who took elocution lessons,
but nonetheless sang me songs

"I didn't go to the moon, I went much further—
for time is the longest distance between two places."

—Tennessee Williams, *The Glass Menagerie*

Acknowledgments

Every effort has been made to trace the ownership of all copyrighted material and to secure the necessary permissions to reprint these selections. In the event of any question arising as to the use of any material, the editor and the publisher, while expressing regret for any inadvertent error, will be happy to make the correction in future printings. Thanks are due to the following for permission to reprint the copyrighted materials listed below:

JAMES AGEE: "A Lullaby," from *The Collected Poems of James Agee*. Copyright © 1968 by the James Agee Trust; used by permission.

B. ALQUIT: "Wandering Chorus," from *Voices Within the Ark*, edited by Howard Schwartz and Anthony Rudolph. Reprinted by permission of the translator, Howard Schwartz.

ANONYMOUS, Hopi: "There!" translated by H. R. Voth, in *Fieldiana: Anthropology*, Vol. 6 No. 1, 1903; Field Museum of Natural History, Chicago. Reprinted by permission of the Field Museum.

ANONYMOUS, Papago: "In the Night," from *Singing for Power: The Song Magic of the Papago Indians of Southern Arizona*, copyright © 1938 by Ruth Murray Underhill. Reprinted by permission of The University of California Press.

ANONYMOUS, Pima: "Song of Creation." Translated from the Pima by Frank Russell in his "The Pima Indians," *Bureau of American Ethnology, 26th Annual Report, 1904–05*, pp. 207–208.

ANONYMOUS, Zuñi: "They Stooped Over and Came Out." Translated from the Zuñi by M. C. Stevenson in her "The Zuñi Indians," *Bureau of American Ethnology, 23rd Annual report, 1901–02*, p. 77.

JORGE LUIS BORGES: "Afterglow," Norman Thomas di Giovanni, translator, from *The New Yorker Book of Poems* (The Viking Press, 1969).

Contents

A Note to the Reader

Life is measured by time. We are here less than an instant in time's constant course of birth and death, the seasons, the mornings, noons, dark nights, and bright dawns of the world. It is the poets who describe immortal moments in our own mortality and help us recall the eternal eternity in which we live, where "Time is the longest distance between two places."

Time Is the
Longest
Distance

There!

There!
There!
Beautiful white-rising has dawned.
Beautiful yellow-rising has dawned.
There!
There!

Hopi

Moon's Ending

Moon, worn thin to the width of a quill,
 In the dawn clouds flying,
How good to go, light into light, and still
 Giving light, dying.

Sara Teasdale (1884–1933)

Watching the moon
at dawn,
solitary, mid-sky,
I knew myself completely,
no part left out.

Izumi Shikibu (10th century)
Translated from the Japanese
by Jane Hirschfield

91

The breeze at dawn has secrets to tell you.
                        Don't go back to sleep.
You must ask for what you really want.
                        Don't go back to sleep.
People are going back and forth across the doorsill
                        where the two worlds touch.
The door is round and open.
                        Don't go back to sleep.

Rumi (1207–1273)
Translated from the Persian
by John Moyne and Coleman Barks

Now Day Is Breaking

Night is ended and the moon
melts in the open sky,
sets in the canals.

September is so alive in this land
of plains, the meadows green
as in southern valleys in spring.
I have left my friends,
hidden my heart inside the ageing walls
to remain alone while I remember you.

How remoter than the moon you are
the day now breaking
and hooves of horses clattering on the stones.

Salvatore Quasimodo (1901–1968)
Translated from the Italian
by Jack Bevan

A Slash of Blue! A sweep of Gray!
Some scarlet patches—on the way—
Compose an evening sky—

A little Purple—slipped between—
Some Ruby Trowsers—hurried on—
A Wave of Gold—a Bank of Day—
This just makes out the Morning sky!

Emily Dickinson (1830–1886)

Song of Creation

I have made the sun!
   I have made the sun!
Hurling it high
   In the four directions
To the east I threw it
   To run its appointed course.

I have made the moon!
   I have made the moon!
Hurling it high
   In the four directions
To the east I threw it
   To run its appointed course.

Pima

There Was a Sound of Airy Seasons Passing

A wry smile cut your face,
gave me deep hurt;
an echo of full agonies
revived as I touched dim
signs of joy on the flesh.

There was a sound of airy seasons passing,
bareness of mornings,
unsteady beams colliding.

Another sun, from which this
weight of silent soliloquy came.

Salvatore Quasimodo (1901–1968)
Translated from the Italian by Jack Bevan

Let me get up early on this summer morning,
without regretting a longer night for repose,

Let me get up early
and let me desire this cold water
for my neck and my face.

Let me watch the bee with envy
in his ceaseless work,
and let me understand it.

Let me get up early and see the boxwood
that probably works as hard as the bee,
and let me be satisfied with that.

Let me get up before the light
and let me know: the day is beginning.

Already, this is victory.

Eugène Guillevic (1907–   )
Translated from the French by Teo Savory

Come morning,
the water brightens
as if by magic.

One moment alive
with thousands of bugs
too small to have names,

Next moment
they're gone,
leaving no trace,

Only the small fish
this way and that
swim in formations.

Han Yü (768–824)
Translated from the Chinese
by Kenneth O. Hanson

Don't shoo the morning flies away
Nor swat mosquitoes in the evening.
Between the two, they fill the world.
So many, should you fight them all?
And yet, how short a time they live.
While they last, give in and let them bite you.
October, and a cold wind wipes them out.
You don't remember then they ever were.

Han Yü (768–824)
Translated from the Chinese
by Kenneth O. Hanson

On New Year's Day, watching it snow

It seemed the plum trees
were already in bloom,
but when I picked a branch
what fell—so much like flowers—
was snow.

If the one I've waited for
came now, what should I do?
This morning's garden filled with snow
is far too lovely
for footsteps to mar.

Izumi Shikibu (10th century)
Translated from the Japanese
by Jane Hirschfield

Nantucket

Friday we found a hollow in the dunes
where only airplanes could see us.
High noon
and the crickets were already chiming.

Zack Rogow (1952–   )

Days Were Great as Lakes

Days were great as lakes
And clear
When we were children.

We sat a long time on their banks
And played,
Or went down to swim
In the fresh water.

And sometimes we wept
In our mother's apron,
For life was filling us
Like jugs of wine.

David Vogel (1891–1943[?])
Translated from the Hebrew
by A. C. Jacobs

From the Most Distant Time

Majestic, from the most distant time,
The sun rises and sets.
Time passes and men cannot stop it.
The four seasons serve them,
But do not belong to them.
The years flow like water.
Everything passes away before my eyes.

The Emperor Wu of Han
[Liang Wu-ti] (464–549)
Translated from the Chinese by
Kenneth Rexroth

Vorobyev Hills

Kisses upon your breast, like water from a jug,
but not forever flows, not ceaseless, summer's spring.
Nor shall we every night raise from the dusty floor
the hurdy-gurdy's roar and stamp and drag our feet.

I've heard about old age. Such terrible forebodings!
Then not a breaker throws its hands up to the stars.
They speak—you don't believe. There's no face in the fields,
there's no heart in the ponds and no god in the wood.

Set your spirit rocking. Splash right through today.
It is the world's midday. Where are your eyes? You see
how thoughts up in the hills are gathered in white bubbles
of woodpeckers and clouds, heat, fircones and pine-needles.

Here the town tram stops: the rails are laid no further.
Beyond, the pines will serve. Beyond they cannot run.
Beyond there's only Sunday. Plucking down the branches,
Running about the glades and slipping through the grass.

Sifting the midday light and the Whit-Sunday crowds,
The copse invites belief the world is always so,
Conceived so by the thickets, suggested to the clearings,
Spilt on us from the clouds, as on a chintz design.

Boris Pasternak (1890–1960)
Translated from the Russian by J. M. Cohen

Tomorrow

And tomorrow the sun will shine again
and on the path I follow
it will unite us again in our happiness
in the midst of this earth which breathes the sun . . .

And to the broad shore, blue with waves,
we shall walk down, slowly and quietly;
we shall look into each other's eyes without a word,
and the wordless silence of happiness will fall over us.

John Henry Mackay (1864–1933)

Drawing by Ronnie C.,
Grade One

For the sky, blue. But the six-year-
old searching his crayon-box, finds
no blue to match that sky
framed by the window—a see-through shine
over treetops, housetops. The wax colors
hold only dead light, not this water-flash
thinning to silver
at morning's far edge.
Gray won't do, either:
gray is for rain that you make with
dark slanting lines down-paper

                        Try orange!

—Draw a large corner circle for sun, egg-yolk solid,
with yellow strokes, leaping outward
like fire bloom—a brightness shouting
flower-shape wind-shape joy-shape!

The boy sighs, with leg-twisting bliss creating . . .

It is done. The stubby crayons
(all ten of them) are stuffed back
bumpily into their box.

                     Ruth Lechlitner (1901–1989)

from *Love Songs from an Ancient Book*

1

I have not seen you, even in dream,
since we parted. The nights descend
on my sleep like heavy clouds.
Suffocated, silenced, I search for you no longer.

My blood has dried in the desert wind.
My heart is humbled. And the morning star
no longer distills its blue and gold,
its honey light upon my trembling eyelids.

But sometimes in that season when the rain
descends and from the dying fields
odors of withering rise at twilight,

the memory of your gentle, innocent voice
awakes my silence with a sound of kindness—
tidings of joy transcending all my days.

Leah Goldberg (1911–1970)
Translated from the Hebrew by Robert Friend

They Stooped Over and Came Out

Our great fathers talked together. Here they arose and
    moved on. They stooped over and came out from the
    fourth world, carrying their precious things clasped to
    their breasts.

They stooped over and came out from moss world, carrying
    their precious things clasped to their breasts.
They stooped over and came out from mud world, carrying
    their precious things clasped to their breasts.
They stooped over and came out from wing world, carrying
    their precious things clasped to their breasts.
They stooped over and came out and saw their Sun Father
    and inhaled the sacred breath of the light of day.

Zuñi

Monte Rio, California

Customers flood the Inn's restaurant
at dinner time. We have to wait for a table.
In the sitting room
a large fish tank's bubbling
but there are no fish.
We take in the view
of the Russian River.
Eight-thirty and it's still sunny.
Hard to believe
that just a couple of months ago
it jumped its banks
but the silt it left
is still on the dock.
The poplar leaves spin
like sequins or seasons.
Tomorrow's the longest day of the year.

Zack Rogow (1952–   )

There's a certain Slant of light,
Winter Afternoons—
That oppresses, like the Heft
Of Cathedral Tunes—

Heavenly Hurt, it gives us—
We can find no scar,
But internal difference,
Where the Meanings, are—

None may teach it—Any—
'Tis the Seal Despair—
An imperial affliction
Sent us of the Air—

When it comes, the Landscape listens—
Shadows—hold their breath—
When it goes, 'tis like the Distance
On the look of Death—

Emily Dickinson (1830–1886)

Early March

1.

   I open the kitchen door:
   someone left the light on.
   No, for the first time this year the sun's
   reflecting off the brick wall
   outside the window.

2.

   At the end of the afternoon
   I walk into my room
   and step on a fire. I jerk
   my foot away, but it isn't burnt.
   I guess for the next few months
   I'll be finding these chips of reddish light
   on the wood floor
   just before nightfall.

Zack Rogow (1952–   )

Almost a Madrigal

The sunflower bends to the west, and day
already sets in its ruined eye,
the air of summer thickens, curves
the leaves, the smoke of the factories.
With the clouds' dry flow, the lightning's screech
this last game of the heavens moves
far-off. Again, love, as for years,
we pause at the changes in the trees
crowded in the circle of the canals.
But it is still our day, and still
that sun that takes its leave
with the thread of its affectionate ray.

I've no more memories, I do not want to remember;
memory rises up from death,
life is without end. Each day
is ours. One day will stop forever,
and you with me, when it seems late for us.
Here on the edge of the canal, our feet
swinging back-and-forth like children's,
let us watch the water, the first branches
in its darkening green.
And the man who approaches in silence
hides no knife within his hands,
but a geranium.

Salvatore Quasimodo (1901–1968)
Translated from the Italian
by Allen Mandelbaum

Wandering Chorus

In the West
circles a wheel
of fire, the glow
of the scarlet
hour.

Shadows
of black loam
rise like a wandering
chorus; the shadow of the East
stands guard
at the far-flung
gates.

And the West pours
red wine
on the white
banner
of silence.

B. Alquit [Eliezer Blum]
(1896–1963)
Translated from the Yiddish
by Howard Schwartz

Autumn Garden

To the ghostly garden, to the silent laurel
Of the green garlands
To the autumn earth
A last farewell!
To the rugged, barren slopes
Reddening in the setting sun,
Distant life cries out
In confusion of harsh sounds:
It cries to the dying sun
That stains the flower beds blood-red.
A flourish of trumpets is heard
Rising piercingly; the river disappears
In the golden sand; silently, their heads turned,
The white statues stand at the end of the bridges:
And things are no more.
Something like a tender, majestic chorus
Of the deep silence
Reaches high, panting, up to my balcony:
And amidst the fragrance of the laurel,
The laurel's lingering, pungent scent,
Among the immortal statues in the sunset
She appears to me, present.

Dino Campana (1885–1932)
Translated from the Italian
by Carlo L. Golino

Blazing in Gold—and
Quenching—in Purple!
Leaping—like Leopards—in the sky—
Then—at the feet of the old Horizon—
Laying its spotted face—to die!

Stooping as low as the kitchen window—
Touching the Roof—
And tinting the Barn—
Kissing its Bonnet to the Meadow—
And the Juggler of Day—is gone!

Emily Dickinson (1830–1886)

Afterglow

Sunset is always disturbing
whether theatrical or muted,
but still more disturbing
is that last desperate glow
that turns the plain to rust
when on the horizon nothing is left
of the pomp and clamor of the setting sun.
How hard holding on to that light, so tautly drawn and
    different,
that hallucination which the human fear of the dark
imposes on space
and which ceases at once
the moment we realize its falsity,
the way a dream is broken
the moment the sleeper knows he is dreaming.

Jorge Luis Borges (1899–1986)
Translated from the Spanish
by Norman Thomas di Giovanni

Evening Comes

Evening comes. My mind is troubled.
I go for a drive past the tombs on the ancient plain.
The beauty of the sunset is heart rending.
The shadows of night come like remembered sorrow.

Li Shang Yin (813[?]–858)
Translated from the Chinese
by Kenneth Rexroth

Dusk

The moon is red in the foggy sky;
in a dancing mist the meadow sleeps
under the reek, and the frogs cry
in the green reeds where a shudder creeps;

the water-lilies close their spathes,
the poplars profile far away,
straight and serried, their vague wraiths;
among the thickets fireflies stray;

the horned owls waken now and row
with heavy wings in silent flight,
the zenith fills with a dull glow.
Pale, Venus comes forth; and it is Night.

Paul Verlaine (1844–1906)
Translated from the French by
C. F. MacIntyre

The Dark and Falling Summer

The rain was full of the freshness
  and the fresh fragrance of darkening grapes.
The rain was as the dark falling of hidden
And fabulous plums ripening—great blue thunderheads
  moving slowly.
The dark air was possessed by the fragrance of freshness,
By a scattered and confused profusion until,
After the tattering began, the pouring-down came,
And plenitude descended, multitudinous.
Everywhere was full of the pulsing of the loud and fallen
  dusk.

Delmore Schwartz (1913–1966)

Toward Myself

The years have made up my face
with memories of love,
adorned my head
with light silver threads
and made me beautiful.

Landscapes are reflected
in my eyes,
the paths I trod
have taught me to walk upright
with beautiful, though tired steps.

If you should see me now,
you would not recognize
the yesterdays you knew.
I go toward myself with a face
you looked for in vain
when I went toward you.

Leah Goldberg (1911–1970)
Translated from the Hebrew
by Robert Friend

The Wind Is from the North

And now at sunset, ripples flecked with gold
Leap lightly over the profounder blue;
The wind is from the north, and days are few
That still divide us from the winter cold.
O, it was easy when the dawn was new
To make the vow that never should be old,
But now at dusk the words are not so bold,—
Thus have I learned. How fares the hour with you?
A heron rises from the trembling sedge,
His vigil at an end. Mine too is done.
A late sail twinkles on the watery edge,
And up the shore lights sparkle one by one.
Seasons will change before tomorrow's sun,
So speaks the dune-grass on the windy ledge.

Robert Hillyer (1895–1961)

The Evening Light Along the Sound

I

As if the sky could no longer hold its color,
that pale blue light sifts down onto the water
like talcum onto a tabletop, or like the fine powder
of memory settling again in the mind in that hour
toward sleep, in that season toward autumn
when the trees begin to fill with a sorrowing air.
Still, there's a moment then when it all seems
so impersonal: no sign that something difficult
is reappearing in our lives, no image
of a feeling, but a feeling itself, like a mis-
directed letter from someone sad and faraway.

II

And it doesn't matter that in that quiet hour
you forget yourself awhile, that the sky
becomes a kind of mirror in which the face
grows dim, then disappears, like a coin
receding underwater. Even the early arrival
of the moon on the horizon only magnifies
the light's desire to turn all things
to light: how quickly it absorbs the sea-
birds drowsing on the air, although, tonight,
the evening star, like a bread-crumb dropped
on the water, is enough to bring them back again.

III

And the night is usually carried in on a breeze,
so that each time the water ripples the light
will darken, as if sprinkled with ash, and become
more fully a part of the air. But the truth is,
the light is sinking into itself, as we, in an absence
of light, will sink back into ourselves—
and it isn't a question, then, of how we feel,
but of how we hold ourselves out to the dark
when the dark closes down around us, and when,
momentarily, what light there is only glitters
in the mind, like a cluster of stars on the Sound.

Sherod Santos (1948–   )

The fireflies wink and glow,
The night is on the march,
The cricket clacks his castanets
And the moon hangs in the larch.
I will take my violin
And a few themes I will play:
Pizzicati for the fireflies,
Harmonics for the moonlight,
And a chord for the smell of hay.

I will play but a few bars,
And when the moon has set
I will listen to the stars.

Robert Hillyer (1895–1961)

Twilight,
and the path you took
coming and going from me
is also gone,
woven closed by spiderwebs and sorrow.

Izumi Shikibu (10th century)
Translated from the Japanese
by Jane Hirschfield

Although there is
not one moment
without longing,
still, how strangely
this autumn twilight fills me.

Ono no Komachi (834–880)
Translated from the Japanese
by Jane Hirschfield

The cicadas sing
in the twilight
of my mountain village—
tonight, no one
will visit save the wind.

Ono no Komachi (834–880)
Translated from the Japanese
by Jane Hirschfield

Twilight of the Outward Life

And children still grow up with longing eyes,
That know of nothing, still grow tall and perish,
And no new traveler treads a better way;

And fruits grow ripe and delicate to cherish
And still shall fall like dead birds from the skies,
And where they fell grow rotten in a day.

And still we feel cool winds on limbs still glowing,
That shudder westward; and we turn to say
Words, and we hear words; and cool winds are blowing

Our wilted hands through autumns of unclutching.
What use is all our tampering and touching?
Why laughter, that must soon turn pale and cry?

Who quarantined our lives in separate homes?
Our souls are trapped in lofts without a skylight;
We argue with a padlock till we die,

In games we never meant to play for keeps.
And yet how much we say in saying: "twilight,"
A word from which man's grief and wisdom seeps

Like heavy honey out of swollen combs.

Hugo von Hofmannsthal (1874–1929)
Translated from the German by Peter Viereck

And Suddenly It's Evening

Each of us is alone on the heart of the earth
pierced by a ray of sun:
and suddenly it's evening.

Salvatore Quasimodo (1901–1968)
Translated from the Italian
by Jack Bevan

Nocturne

A long arm embossed with gold slides from the tree tops
And starts to come down and jingle in the branches.
Leaves and flowers crowd together and understand each
   other.
I have seen the glass snake glide through the evening quiet.
Diana leans over the pond and puts on her mask.
A satin slipper runs in the glade
Like a call from the sky which reaches the horizon.
The boats of night are ready to go.

Other people will come to sit on the iron chair.
Other people will watch it when I am no longer here.
The night will forget the ones who loved it so much.
Never a call will come to light up our faces again,
Never a sob to bring back our love.
Our windows will be put out.
A couple of foreigners will walk along the gray street.
Voices.
Other voices will sing, other eyes weep.

In a new house
Everything will be consummated, everything will be forgiven.
There will be fresh trouble and a new forest,
And maybe someday, for those other friends—
God will hold out the happiness he promised us once.

Léon-Paul Fargue (1876–1947)
Translated from the French by Kenneth Rexroth

Evening

Evening's barefoot monk
descends from the church on the hill
his long shadow falls
across the empty market place.

The turtledoves in the dovecote
murmur to each other sleepily
and our house breathes the peace
and piousness
of ryebread and evensong.

Itzik Manger (1901–1969)
Translated from the Yiddish
by Miriam Waddington

In Evening Air

I

A dark theme keeps me here,
Though summer blazes in the vireo's eye.
Who would be half possessed
By his own nakedness?
Waking's my care—
I'll make a broken music, or I'll die.

II

Ye littles, lie more close!
Make me, O Lord, a last, a simple thing
Time cannot overwhelm.
Once I transcended time
A bud broke to a rose,
And I rose from a last diminishing.

III

I look down the far light
And I behold the dark side of a tree
Far down a billowing plain,
And when I look again,
It's lost upon the night—
Night I embrace, a dear proximity.

IV

I stand by a low fire
Counting the wisps of flame, and I watch how
Light shifts upon the wall.
I bid stillness be still.
I see, in evening air,
How slowly dark comes down on what we do.

Theodore Roethke (1908–1963)

This Evening

Evening in the house
where you sit and look out
the window,
and in her chair your wife is knitting
or maybe sewing.
You turn around—and she is sitting there
doing nothing,
the needle, scissors, cloth
are lying idle in her hands,
and she is lost in thought over the days and days
that creep by in worries.
Here, we say, everything is always missing
and the daily grind is inescapable.
And every day that's gone is gone for good,
it won't come back again.
And just as this one has, the next too will pass,
and what was hoped for, waited for,
will also have gone past.

These are the things she is thinking,
when she looks up hopefully at you—
who have just now turned from the window
to look at her.
Everything suddenly is clear.
You get up
and go over to your wife, your faithful wife,
and touch her shoulder lightly
and stroke her hair,
and want to say so many sweet things to her,
and say not a single word.
You go back to your chair
and look out the window.
The night is deep, the stars are big,
and quietly your heart opens.

Zishe Landau (1889–1937)
Translated from the Yiddish
by Irving Feldman

An Open Arc

Evening shatters in the earth
with thunder of smoke and the owl
beats out "tu," telling only
of silence. The high dark islands
crush down the sea; on the beach
night enters inside the shells. And you
measure the future, the beginning
no longer here, part and slowly break up
the sum of a time already missing.
As the foam clings to the stones you lose the sense
of the ruin's impassive flow.
The closed song of the owl
knows no death as it dies,
feels around in its hunt for love, continues
an open arc, reveals
its solitude. Someone will come.

Salvatore Quasimodo (1901–1968)
Translated from the Italian
by Jack Bevan

At Sunset

Through joy and sorrow we have
walked hand in hand;
we are resting from our wandering
now above the quiet countryside.

Around us the valleys slope away;
already the air is growing dark,
only two larks are left climbing
into the haze, dreaming of the night.

Come near and let them flutter;
soon it will be time to sleep,
lest we should lose our way
in this solitude.

O broad, still peace.
So deep in the sunset,
how tired of wandering we are—
could this perhaps be death?

Joseph von Eichendorff (1788–1857)

Snow on Lotus Mountain

Sunset. Blue peaks vanish in dusk.
Under the Winter stars
My lonely cabin is covered with snow.
I can hear the dogs barking
At the rustic gate.
Through snow and wind
Someone is coming home.

Liu Ch'ang Ch'ing (709–780)
Translated from the Chinese
by Kenneth Rexroth

VI

The white moonglow
shines on the trees;
from each bough
a voice flees
as the leaves move . . .

Oh, my love.

The pond reflects,
a mirror deep,
the black silhouette
of the willow tree
where the wind weeps . . .

Oh, reverie.

Now a tender
and vast appeasement
seems to descend
from the firmament
with the irised star . . .

Ah, exquisite hour.

Paul Verlaine (1844–1906)
Translated from the French
by C. F. MacIntyre

Night Garden With Ladies

They are busy in the moon
whispering, laughing

digging around the tulips,
the roses. They have round

faces, heavy bodies; they
wear cotton stockings

and take a long time standing
up again. Their tools lean

in apron pockets; heavy sweaters
on in the cool air, their faces

streaked from work in the night
earth, I know them well,

their dark competence. They
are my aunts, my three grandmothers,

and their talk with each turn
of the trowel is of the cousins,

our fates. They are relentless,
yet say they want success,

happiness. They treat all the roots
alike, and when the sky

becomes light green and the trees
lift themselves from blackness,

they move off into the air,
their arms up, hair flying after.

Dona Stein (1935–   )

In the Discreet Splendor

In the discreet splendor of the moonlight,
my room dreams towards me. At my head,
a white and slender sentinel stands. The candle,
its light extinguished by a breath of night,
glows with a radiance that is the moon's.

A. L. Strauss (1892–1953)
Translated from the Hebrew
by Robert Friend

In the Night

In the night
The rain comes down.
Yonder at the edge of the earth
There is a sound like cracking,
There is a sound like falling.
Down yonder it goes on slowly rumbling.
It goes on shaking.

Papago

Although the wind
blows terribly here,
the moonlight also leaks
between the roof planks
of this ruined house.

Izumi Shikibu (10th century)
Translated from the Japanese
by Jane Hirschfield

Night deepens
with the sound
of a calling deer,
and I hear
my own one-sided love.

Ono no Komachi (834–880)
Translated from the Japanese
by Jane Hirschfield

A Lullaby

Sleep, child, lie quiet, let be:
Now like a still wind, a great tree,
Night upon this city moves
Like leaves, our hungers and our loves.

Sleep, rest easy, while you may.
Soon it is day.

And elsewhere likewise love is stirred;
Elsewhere the speechless song is heard:
Wherever children sleep or wake
Souls are lifted, hearts break.

Sleep, be careless while you can.
Soon you are man.

And everywhere good men contrive
Good reasons not to be alive.
And even should they build their best
No man could bear tell you the rest.

Sleep child, for your parents' sake.
Soon you must wake.

James Agee (1909–1955)

In the Night

Out of my window late at night I gape
And see the stars but do not watch them really,
And hear the trains but do not listen clearly;
Inside my mind I turn about to keep
Myself awake, yet am not there entirely;
Something of me is out in the dark landscape.

How much am I then what I think, how much what I feel,
How much the eye that seems to keep stars straight?
Do I control what I can contemplate
Or is it my vision that's amenable?
I turn in my mind; my mind is a room whose wall
I can see the top of but never completely scale.

All that I love is, like the night, outside,
Good to be gazed at, looking as if it could
With a simple gesture be brought inside my head,
Or in my heart, but my thoughts about it divide
Me from my object. Now, deep in my bed,
I turn and the world turns on the other side.

Elizabeth Jennings (1926–   )

The way I must enter
leads through darkness to darkness—
O moon above the mountains' rim,
please shine a little farther
on my path.

Izumi Shikibu (10th century)
Translated from the Japanese
by Jane Hirschfield

(This is believed to have been Shikibu's final poem, written on her deathbed.)

Our share of night to bear—
Our share of morning—
Our blank in bliss to fill
Our blank in scorning—

Here a star, and there a star,
Some lose their way!
Here a mist, and there a mist,
Afterwards—Day!

Emily Dickinson (1830–1886)

In This Deep Darkness

In this deep heavy darkness
remember me who stood before you—
thirty-two years, to the day,
in this deep heavy darkness.

Remember me when you climb the watchtower
at evening in a bloody swirl of light.
Remember me when you drive away the clouds
from this world down into another

where clouds vanish and are forgotten.
Remember me among your flocks;
remember me more than you remember all your orphans
in this deep heavy darkness

where I am lost more than an orphan,
more than a lamb, for my eyes are open
and I see how the blue darkens. I am not deceived:
I see how blood thickens, the voice stumbles,

how at evening everything rises and returns
with its memories, and is a mouth to all
that has ever been since time's beginning,
all that is forever homeless
in this deep heavy darkness.

Natan Zach (1930–   )
Translated from the Hebrew
by Peter Ererwine and Shula Starkman

This Night

This night and all its silence
this night
and these three stars
lost among trees
this wind

this wind
that has stopped to listen
to this night
this night
and these three stars
this wind

Leah Goldberg (1911–1970)
Translated from the Hebrew
by Robert Friend

At the New Year

In the shape of this night, in the still fall
    of snow, Father
In all that is cold and tiny, these little birds
    and children
In everything that moves tonight, the trolleys
    and the lovers, Father
In the great hush of country, in the ugly noise
    of our cities
In this deep throw of stars, in those trenches
    where the dead are, Father
In all the wide land waiting, and in the liners
    out on the black water
In all that has been said bravely, in all that is
    mean anywhere in the world, Father
In all that is good and lovely, in every house
    where sham and hatred are
In the name of those who wait, in the sound
    of angry voices, Father
Before the bells ring, before this little point in time
    has rushed us on
Before this clean moment has gone, before this night
    turns to face tomorrow, Father
There is this high singing in the air
Forever this sorrowful human face in eternity's window
And there are other bells that we would ring, Father
Other bells that we would ring.

Kenneth Patchen (1911–1972)

The heart of man has four chambers, and each is filled with
    tremors in the spring.
The season of summer insinuates with song and evidences of
    fertility,
Whereas the autumn, by incendiary measures, inflames the
    woods and demonstrates how it is possible to grow old
    without loss of beauty.
Winter, with its stern outlook and its northern bearing, merely
    underscores the warmth of the ordinary bed.

The earth can usually be relied upon to conspire and assist,
    performing as mutual friend,
And the moon will always be in character.
The planet, busy as it is between this solstice and the next,
    helps out a man and woman; and the race continues.

Norman Corwin (1910–   )

INDEX OF AUTHORS

INDEX OF TITLES

INDEX OF FIRST LINES